Allen Johnson

The intendant as a political agent under Louis XIV

Allen Johnson

The intendant as a political agent under Louis XIV

ISBN/EAN: 9783337134471

Printed in Europe, USA, Canada, Australia, Japan

Cover: Foto ©Suzi / pixelio.de

More available books at **www.hansebooks.com**

THE INTENDANT AS A POLITICAL AGENT UNDER LOUIS XIV.

Submitted in partial fulfilment of the requirements for the degree of Doctor of Philosophy, in the Faculty of Political Science, Columbia University.

BY

ALLEN JOHNSON, A. M.

Associate Professor of History, Iowa College.
Sometime Fellow in European History, Columbia University.

LOWELL, MASS.
COURIER-CITIZEN COMPANY, PRINTERS.
1899.

TABLE OF CONTENTS.

INTRODUCTION.

As one turns the leaves of the voluminous administrative correspondence of the old régime and reads here and there, his first impression is that of prodigious activity amid bewildering diversity and complexity. The pages are crowded with obscure allusions to peculiar local customs; dignitaries of more or less importance appear and disappear; titles and offices multiply to distraction. The student is tempted to believe the old régime a chaos. It is not long, however, before the figure of one administrative officer emerges with tolerable clearness; the *intendant* seems omnipresent. And yet, when one attempts to give definiteness to his duties, chaos threatens to reign again. There is something vexingly elusive about the intendant. Viewed from one point, he is the submissive creature of the *contrôleur*; viewed in another light, he seems to rule as absolutely as the great monarch himself. Whether he is overwhelmed with popular applause in Pau or cursed with virulent fury in Poitou, the old régime is inseparably associated with his name.

The difficulty of putting the intendant's duties into precise form arises largely from the habit of regarding him as an administrative officer, pure and simple, when it should be borne in mind that the intendant was peculiarly *hors de loi*. He was bound by no established administrative statutes or regulations; not even his commission was registered in Parlement. To the local authorities he owed no obedience, since local laws and *coutumes* had crystalized centuries before the intendant became a part of the administrative organism. He received frequent instructions from the king in council and from the ministers, it is true, but in general he was left singularly free to exercise his discretion. Given the ends in view, he was nearly always permitted to choose the means best suited to reach them. Such freedom might have proved inimical to the interests of the crown, if the intendant had not been brought into immediate touch with the royal council and with the chief ministers of state by a minute and regular correspondence. This intimate connection made him responsive to the slightest wish of the king,—made him in fact the supple, subservient agent of royalty for the gratification of its every whim. When the crown felt itself menaced from any quarter and was forced to act with the full weight of its authority, a trusted officer was at hand to secure obedience to its behests. The last word upon the great historical movements of "le grand siècle" will not be said until full credit is accorded to the intendants for their unceasing labors in behalf of absolutism.

Few thoughtful readers have laid aside De Tocqueville's brilliant review of the intendants without a desire to know more of the men who have exercised so profound an influence upon French institutions. In the following pages an attempt has been made to illustrate the nature of the intendant's office by selecting the more important phases of his activity in a period when the social and political fabric of the old régime was assuming its permanent form. The picture must necessarily be defective. De Tocqueville has remarked with pardonable exaggeration that under the old régime the government took the place of Providence. The student who has followed the tortuous course of the government under Louis XIV. will be inclined to acquiesce in this sentiment; assuredly the ways of that government seem often as inscrutable as those of Providence.

The writer gladly takes this opportunity to acknowledge his indebtedness to Professor James Harvey Robinson of Columbia University for many helpful suggestions, and to Mr. George H. Baker, Librarian of the Columbia College Library, for repeated favors. Thanks are due also to the authorities of the Harvard College Library for their kind attentions.

GRINNELL, IOWA, Dec. 26th, 1898.

THE INTENDANT AS A POLITICAL AGENT
UNDER LOUIS XIV.

CHAPTER I.

ORIGIN AND CHARACTERISTICS OF THE OFFICE OF
INTENDANT.

There is no more persistent error among historians than that
which ascribes to Cardinal Richelieu the creation of the institution
of the intendants. The source of the error is clear enough. In
the collection known as *anciennes lois françaises* occurs an edict
of the year 1635, which the editor has dubbed "*Édit de Création
des Intendants.*" The name *intendant* appears in connection with
several financial offices, either newly created or reorganized, and
the editor seems to have jumped at the conclusion that he had
before him a document actually creating the institution so familiar
to students of the old régime. The blunder was detected many
years ago, but historians continue to perpetuate the illusion. It is
comparatively easy to show that the word *intendant* in the edict of
1635 is to be understood in a totally different sense from that of
the same word used in the phrase *intendant de justice;* and it is
still easier to prove that intendants were in existence before the
year 1635.[*] The former line of evidence has been restated too
often to need reiteration here, but the latter may be profitably
reviewed.

The first intendant of whom record is preserved is Pierre

[*]See Caillet: *De l'Administration en France*, I. pp. 71 et seq. This work, published
in 1857, proved beyond a doubt that the edict of 1635 did not create the office of intendant,
but simply created, or altered the nature of, certain officers known as *présidents et trésoriers généraux des finances.*
    M. Hanotaux cites an instance where certain *présidents* and *trésoriers* at Montpellier
styled themselves *intendants des gabelles* Hanotaux: *Les origines des Intendants,* p. 2.
    Even in the time of Louis XIV, we find numerous instances of the title used in its
most general sense, where no reference to the royal intendant or *commissaire departi* is
intended.

Panisse, who was commissioned about the year 1555 to go to Corsica as *intendant de justice*.* The island had recently fallen into the possession of the French and the king desired to establish order there by means of a royal agent. To this end Panisse—"nostre amé et féal conseiller Président en nostre court des Généraulx de la Justice des Aydes à Montpellier"—was given "plain pouvoir, auctorité, commission et mandement spécial" to confer with the lieutenant-governor and to summon in assembly the notables and officials of the island. He was to learn from them the customs, laws and usages in the administration of justice. Over all courts he was to have "la superintendance générale," and his regulative ordinances were to be final "comme s'ilz avaient esté ou estaient donnez par l'une de noz courts de Parlement." He was to go about from town to town to inform himself in regard to the local laws and customs and to exercise such police powers as he deemed necessary. The conduct of civil officers was to be noted "dillegemment, secrètement et bien." He might even suspend them from office, if occasion demanded. Officers of finance were to be subjected to the same scrutiny. All abuses were to be reported to the *conseil privé*; although in urgent cases the intendant might undertake their correction upon consultation with the governor.

The essential character of the institution and the lines of its future development are indicated in this commission.† The intendant is to represent the king in matters of justice, police, and finance in parts of the realm where war had almost subverted the social order. He is completely dependent upon the royal will in regard to both appointment and tenure of office; he is essentially the king's man. And yet, from the very nature of the circumstances that make his office necessary, he possesses, and must possess, no little discretionary power to encounter successfully the opposition which the faithful performance of his duties will inevitably arouse.

The links in the chain that binds the first intendants to those of the time of Richelieu may be easily supplied. The admirable exposition of M. Hanotaux‡ has done much to make the connec-

---

* Hanotaux: *Pièces just.* I. p. 179.
† "Elle est comme un raccourci de toute l'institution dont elle est la première ébauche." Hanotaux, p. 23.
‡ Hanotaux: *Origines des Intendants.*

tion intelligible, and all students of the institutions of the old régime will gladly acknowledge their indebtedness to his work.

During the years of civil war in France, when the royal power was reduced to a mere shadow, there are few records of intendants actually bearing the title. Royal commissioners were numerous, but their functions are not to be confounded with those of the intendants of succeeding years, however much the practice of commissioning such royal agents may have contributed to the final triumph of the system of permanent intendancies. The office of royal commissioner was ill-defined; his authority was vague and transitory.[*]

With the revival of the monarchy under Henry IV. the intendants spring into new prominence, and for obvious reasons. Two gigantic tasks confronted Henry of Navarre: he had first to conquer the land of which he was only grudgingly named king; and then, task scarcely less onerous, he had to pacify and rehabilitate his kingdom. It was no easy matter to stay the hand of the rough soldier who had helped to win the allegiance of some rebellious province and who now lusted after the spoils of victory; nor, on the other hand, to provide for the legitimate needs of the army of occupation, without kindling once more the hatred of the newly regained province. Due regard for the support of the soldiers had to be joined with generous respect for the feelings of the people. The conditions were unusual and fully justified the plan adopted by the king.[†] By the side of the governor of a province and the commander of the army of pacification was placed an officer bearing a royal mandate which conferred upon him extraordinary powers within the province where the army was to operate. In nearly every instance he bore the title of intendant, but with certain phrases added to indicate the particular duties for which he was commissioned. He might be *"intendant de justice"* in an army and act as counselor to the general in matters relating to the preservation of order and discipline among the soldiers. He might be charged with the *"intendance des finances"* in an army and have supervision of the moneys raised for the support of the troops, or he might combine all these duties and be styled *"Intendant de justice, de police, des vivres et des finances"*

* Hanotaux, pp. 31-35.
† Hanotaux, pp. 41 et seq.

in a specified army. In each and every case the sphere of his influence and power was the province where the army of pacification was located.

The transformation of the intendant of an army into the intendant of a province was only natural. It might often happen that an intendant would remain for a time in the province after the immediate occasion for his coming had passed away. He would then almost imperceptibly become *intendant de province.*[*] Here, then, was a tendency which, had it not been retarded by the activity of the government in other affairs, might have made the intendancy what it became in the reign of Louis XIV., a permanent office. By the year 1598, the first task of Henry had been achieved; he could then fairly claim to be master of his kingdom and could begin with confidence the economic and financial restoration of France. Sure of the support of magistrates and people, the king could now dispense with the intendants. They had not yet acquired enough stability to exist after the immediate needs to which they owed their existence had been met. If they did not entirely disappear, they became so few as to escape notice. For the re-establishment of order in the finances, which now became the chief concern of Henry and his minister Sully, recourse was had once more to royal commissioners, who have erroneously been confounded with the intendants, because the term intendant was sometimes applied to them in contemporary documents. The error is of exactly the same sort as that in regard to the edict of 1635. *Intendant* is used in a general sense to designate a class of officers with supervisory powers, not the particular agent whom we have met as *intendant de justice.*[†]

The death of Henry IV. left France once more a prey to the decentralizing forces which he had overcome with so much difficulty. The regency grasped desperately at the only means which would preserve its own existence: the revival of the intendants. Many of the old intendants were recommissioned; new ones were appointed until there was hardly a disaffected province where the royal power was not represented in the person of an intendant. Commissions varied between different intendants in different provinces, and between intendants who succeeded one another in the same province, but the tendency was to unite the various appellations in the collective title *intendant de justice, police et finances.*"*

When Cardinal Richelieu came into power he found little to add to the powers and attributes of the intendants. Not only was the institution in existence before his day, but it had approved itself to all who sympathized with the efforts of royalty to make head against the forces of disintegration within the realm. It cannot be said that the great cardinal added anything new to the institution of the intendants; their powers remained essentially the same; and yet Richelieu undoubtedly exercised over the intendants an influence which may have been transitory but which was very real, so long as his master mind directed the state. The intense activity of the great minister manifested itself by a sort of reflex action in the intendants, who were fast developing into vital organs of the government. The intendancies were multiplied, and to the tenure of office was given a greater relative permanence; new men were appointed who exercised their powers with an energy and decision that seemed to transform the nature of their office. Conscious of the entire support of the central government, these intendants bent all their efforts to abase the ancient local authorities. They lived in constant conflict with the governors of provinces, with the local magistrates, and with the provincial parlements and courts. It was at bottom only one phase of that deeper struggle between absolutism and the vestiges of local government. The conflict between the parlements and the intendants was long and bitter, continuing well into the reign of Louis XIV.

Enough has been said, surely, to prove that Richelieu did not "create" the intendants; all evidence goes to prove that the institution was a growth. It will be a matter of surprise to those who have regarded the intendants as the peculiar product of Richelieu's genius, to find how little value he attached to the office. In his political writings there is nothing to indicate that he regarded the intendants as permanent organs of the administration, or that he rated their temporary usefulness very highly. On the contrary, if the words of the "*Testament politique*" are to be taken as his own, he entertained so poor an opinion of the institution that he

---

* Hanotaux, pp. 211 et seq.

actually favored reducing their powers to those of ordinary commissioners.*

How firmly the intendants had entrenched themselves in the provinces, and how jealously the local authorities guarded the remains of their ancient power, the demands of the Fronde in 1648 attest. One of the first concessions that the court party had to make was the revocation of the intendants; all intendancies, except those in six provinces†, were summarily suppressed. It was a great victory for particularism over absolutism. "La cour," cried the notorious Cardinal de Retz exultantly, "La cour se sentit toucher à la prunelle de l'œil par la suppression des intendances."‡

The revival of the monarchy under Louis XIV. was accompanied by a gradual restoration of intendancies, so that by the year 1698 they numbered twenty-six, and at the outbreak of the Revolution thirty-three, besides six in the colonies. The generalities varied both in number and extent during the reign of Louis XIV.‖ Picardy and Artois, for example, were for a long time under the same intendant. Certain conquered provinces were governed by intendants, but not created into generalities for several years.§ Generalities were designated indifferently by the name of the chief town and by the name of the province in which the greater portion of the generality lay; the generality was not necessarily coextensive with the province.

It seems to have been a common practice to choose intendants from among the *maîtres des requêtes*, who were usually representatives of the petty nobility.¶ They were the people of whom St. Simon said, "Ces avocats renforcés et qui du barreau,

---

* "Je crois qu'il sera très utile d'envoyer souvent dans les provinces des conseillers d'Etat ou des maîtres des requêtes bien choisis, non seulement pour faire la fonction d'intendant de justice dans les villes capitales, ce qui peut plus servir à leur vanité qu'à utilité du public; mais pour aller en tous lieux des provinces;" etc., etc. *Testament politique*, pp. 161-162. (Edition of 1689.)

† Bourgogne, Provence, Lyonnais, Languedoc, Champagne, Picardie.

‡ Isambert, XVII. pp. 72, 73.

Intendance is the term usually applied to the office; *généralité* is used to denote the territorial division administered by the intendant. Later the term *intendance* was also used in this latter sense. I have taken the liberty of anglicizing these terms.

§ e. g. Bourgogne with Bresse, Gex, and Bugey.

* Not a few of the attributes given to the intendants seem to have been borrowed from these *maître des requêtes*, whose lineal descent from the *missi dominici* of Charlemagne and from the *enquêteurs* of Louis IX. and Philip III. has been insisted upon rather too positively by some historians. These *maîtres des requêtes* were assigned to regular circuits for the purpose of securing the enforcement of royal ordinances and of supervising the administration of justice. The *Code Michaud* of 1629 [Isambert, XVI. p. 223] gives their duties in detail. Besides supervisory powers, they are to have power to reform the taxes and their assessment, to inspect registers and rolls, and to repress

où ils gagnaient leur vie il n'y a pas longtemps, sont devenus des magistrats considérables, ont pris le *de*."*
It was part of the policy of Louis XIV. to choose his ministers and officers of state from the lower nobility, who could never detract from his glory or rival his influence. The young man who aspired to become intendant smoothed the way to that responsible post by the purchase of a commission as *maitre des requêtes*. It would have been contrary to the practice of the times if intrigue and favoritism had not played a prominent part in the appointment of intendants. Certain intendancies were more lucrative than others; they varied greatly, too, in responsibility and dignity. The term of service in an intendancy was not fixed. There was no attempt at uniformity, for the essential feature of the office was its elasticity and its complete dependence upon the will of the king. At Rouen there were twenty-one intendants from 1664 to 1716, no one of whom held office for more than seven years, while ten of them held office for less than three. In Languedoc, between the years 1672 and 1718, there were only two intendants; of these one held office twelve, the other thirty-three years. Four intendants were installed in Picardy between 1664 and 1718, holding office nine, ten, fourteen and ten years, respectively. Transfers from one intendancy to another were frequent, and were dictated by various motives. In 1665 Colbert seems to have made a change "*quasy général*" of intendants, removing certain incumbents for the benefit of new appointees.† Pinon, Vicomte de Quincy, was successively intendant at Pau, Alençon, Poitiers, and Dijon. De Bouville passed from Limoges to Alençon; he returned then to Limoges and some years later assumed the intendancy of Orléans. Whatever may have been the immediate occasion for such frequent changes, they promoted zeal and assiduity in office and made the intendant completely subservient to the royal will. The office never became a sinecure.

Cases of absolute removal seem to have been comparatively few. Larcher‡ was recalled from the intendancy of Chalons, apparently for neglect of duty through repeated absences, but he

summarily all abuses and all attempts to evade the royal ordinances. Their ordinances were to be regarded as final, with appeal only to the council of the King. With the rise of the intendants, their powers must have been greatly restricted.
* Monin: *Hist. admin. du Languedoc pendant l'intendance de Basville*, p. 1.
† *Journal d'Ollivier d'Ormesson*, II. p. 421 et seq.
‡ Boislisle: *Correspondance des intendants*, II. No. 41.

afterward became President of the *chambre des comptes* at Paris. When D'Arguesseau showed lack of necessary firmness for the responsible intendancy of Languedoc, he was quietly recalled to the *conseil d'État*, of which he was a member, and Basville was made his successor.* And even when Marillac was recalled from Poitou in disgrace he soon regained favor and was given another intendancy.

The old feudal tendency for offices to become heritable crops out occasionally in the efforts of certain intendants to secure the succession in office to their sons. When a father had proved his efficiency by long years of service, his petition was sometimes granted. After twenty years of service in the intendancy of Provence, Lebret was succeeded by his son, who had been for several years associated with him. De Bouville pressed the project of creating a new generality of Chartres, in the hope that he might be transferred thither and so be near his son, who, he fondly hoped, would be given the intendancy of Alençon. If his son were thought too young, he offered to assume both intendancies until the young man acquired the necessary experience for so responsible a post.† The project fell through, but the younger Bouville subsequently became intendant at Alençon. Such cases became more frequent in the following century, when, for example, three generations of the Chauvelin family succeeded with a single break to the intendancy of Picardy.‡

The government of Louis XIV. expressed no objection to plurality of offices, so that many intendants retained their position even after they had been appointed *conseillers d'État*. Lebret was intendant of Provence and also first president of the Parlement of Aix.§ If the intendant was spurred to assiduity in office by the fear of removal or transference, he was perhaps no less influenced by the hope of reward. His ardent ambition was a place in the *conseil a' État*. "Après vingt années d'absence de Paris," wrote one intendant to the *contrôleur*, "pendant laquelle j'ay tasché de ne rien omettre pour l'exécution des ordres de S. M., avec une fidélité et un désintéressement que j'ose dire avoir esté sans réserve, souf-

---

* Monin, pp. 2, 3.
† Boislisle, II. No. 875.
‡ Boyer de Ste. Suzanne: *Les intendants de la généralité d'Amiens, Appendice.*
§ Marchand, pp. 20 et seq.

frez-moy la liberté de vous demander l'honneur de vostre protection, en cas de quelque vacance de place au Conseil. Encore que M. de Marillac, qui me succéda à l'intendance de Poitiers, soit aujourd'huy le premier montant des conseillers d'Estat semestres, et qu'il semble que je doive peu espérer, après que tant de personnes moins âgées que moy et moins anciennes dans l'employ ont esté placées, si j'ay le bonheur de vous voir persuadé en ma faveur, je ne déspéreray point d'un moment heureux qui me donne la consolation qu'ont eue les sieurs des Hameaux et de Miroménil, mes deux oncles, de mourir conseiller d'Estat."*

The salary of the intendant varied with the importance of the generality to which he was assigned. De Breteuil at Amiens received a yearly income of 12,000 livres,† while de Bouville at Orléans received 18,300 livres.‡ An allowance of 100 livres per month was also made for the intendant's secretary.§ The intendants were the recipients of many perquisites. Upon appointment of his successor in the intendancy of Dauphiné, Boucher received as an annual pension the 6,000 livres which he had drawn regularly for fourteen years as a "gratification."‖

The intendants were not troubled by excessive modesty. When Le Gendre at Montauban wrote to thank the contrôleur for a pension accorded his sub-delegate, he unblushingly requested a similar pension to reimburse himself for numerous expenses which he recounted at some length. The colossal effrontery of the man appears in the closing passages of this precious missive: "Vous savez que je suis seul dans cette province, et que, si je ne soutenois pas le caractère dont vous m'avez revêtu avec un peu de dignité, cela pourroit diminuer la considération que vous aimez que vos créatures [sic] s'attirent; et peut-être que le Roi n'en seroit pas si bien servi. Quoique je sois un des plus pauvres intendants du royaume, j'aime mieux manger mon bien, n'étant pas possible que mon revenu, joint aux seuls appointements d'intendant, puisse suffire aux dépenses que je suis obligé de faire, quoique bien réglées, que de ne pas vivre avec honneur dans la place où

---

* Boislisle, I. No. 568. Shortly after this same intendant asked for the position of first president of the Parlement of Rouen.
† Boyer de Ste. Suzanne, p. 388.
‡ Boislisle, II. No. 875 note.
§ Boyer de Ste. Suzanne, p. 388.
Boislisle, I. No. 810.
Boislisle, I. No. 784. A similar pension was awarded to Basville. The assembly of Bresse gave a gratification of 1600 livres to the intendant. Boislisle, I. No. 169 note.

vous m'avez mis. Je prends la liberté de vous présenter sur cela un placet, dans lequel j'expose mon état au naturel; je vous supplie de vouloir bien en parler au Roi, quand vous le trouverez à propos. Je mets toute ma confiance en vos bontés. La moindre pension, qui seroit pour moi un glorieux titre d'honneur, me mettroit en état de ne point déranger mes affaires en exécutant vos ordres, et feroit connoître au public que vous êtes content de mes services. C'est où je borne toute mon ambition."* The response of the *contrôleur* was, "La conjoncture n'est pas favorable pour obtenir une pension." But it should be added in all fairness that many intendants had to rely on other sources of income besides their salary, to meet the expenses which their social duties imposed upon them.†

As the absolute monarchy came to meddle more and more with the local concerns of the provinces, the duties of the intendants became more numerous and exacting. It was often a physical impossibility for an intendant properly to inform himself of the state of the different parishes of his generality, much less to secure the enforcement of ordinances designed to reach disorders in them. He was obliged to rely on helpers, and in most cases he sought men of influence in their communities, to whom he might safely delegate his authority in exigencies that arose. This practice of sub-delegating, at first resorted to only as special occasion required,‡ received the tacit approval of the *conseil* and speedily became universal. It was, of course, open to grave abuses. An intendant who was disposed to make his office a sinecure might employ a small army of sub-delegates to attend to the irksome details of his office. Such cases, indeed, were not wanting. "Je ne puis pas m'empescher," wrote Colbert to an intendant in 1674, "de vous donner avis que ce qui fait le plus de peine au Roy sur tout ce qui regarde la conduite de MM. les commissaires départis dans les provinces,§ c'est le nombre de subdélegués qu'ils establissent dans tous les lieux de leurs départements, lesquels s'attribuent, de leur chef, l'autorité de prendre connoissance de toutes sortes d'affaires, et qui abusent très-souvent d'un pouvoir

---

* Boislisle, II. No. 1145. A similar request in Boislisle, I. No. 810.
† Boislisle, II. No. 1143.
‡ *Lettres de Colbert*, IV. p. 108, No. 99.
§ The formula almost invariably used in official documents of the old régime to designate the intendants.

qu'ils ne connoissent pas, et qu'ils estendent autant que leurs fantaisies, leurs passions, et leurs intérests leur suggèrent."[*] On the other hand, it should be said that there were intendants who displayed indefatigable zeal, employing sub-delegates only as absolute necessity required.[†] Instances are not wanting where intendants showed a rare amount of self-denial in the performance of burdensome duties which could not be intrusted to other hands.

Many considerations entered into the choice of sub-delegates, particularly when the office became firmly established. While it was essential to have men who enjoyed consideration and respect in their communities, and men who possessed tact and aptitude for their duties, it was no less important that the sub-delegates should be staunchly loyal to the king's interests. When this latter condition was satisfied there was thought to be no incompatibility in holding simultaneously the office of sub-delegate and a local office. *Consuls* were often sub-delegates;[‡] *syndics*, and occasionally mayors, retained both offices.[§] Lebret declared (in 1704) that all his sub-delegates were "*gens de justice.*"[‖] It was no uncommon thing for the clergy to act in this capacity.[¶] Yet this union of royal office and local office was watched with suspicion by the people. The *tiers état* of Béarn protested vigorously when their syndic became also a sub-delegate. They insisted that he resign one office or the other, and they seem to have carried their point.[**]

A common practice was that of choosing a sub-delegate-general, who, upon commission from the king, discharged the duties of the intendant during the latter's enforced absence.[°] In Pau, precedent seems to have designated the First President of the Parlement for sub-delegate-general of that generality, but in one case, at least, the choice fell upon a counselor of the Parlement. There was probably no established precedent elsewhere.

---

* *Lettres de Colbert*, IV. p. 198, No. 98.
† Marchand, pp. 55, 56. Lebret boasted that he had but one sub-delegate, but he certainly employed others for special purposes.
‡ Boislisle, II. No. 1060.
§ Boislisle, II. No. 1112. Boislisle, II. No. 274.
‖ Boislisle, II. No. 569.
¶ Boislisle, I. No. 1747.
Marchand, p. 56. "Une liste de subdélégués [of Provence] serait extrêmement variée; on y trouverait non seulement des magistrats, mais des hommes d'épée et même des hommes d'église."
* Boislisle, II. No. 1112.
° Boyer de Ste. Suzanne, p. 29.
† Boislisle, II. No. 701. Where illness or other cause prevented the intendant from

The edict of 1704 which made the sub-delegate a regular officer of the administration probably brought about no radical change in the office aside from greater fixedness. The ostensible motive for this step appears in the preamble: "Le ministère de ces employés est devenu sy important et leurs fonctions sy étendues, que nous avons jugé à propos d'investir ceux quy les exerceront à l'advenir, d'un caractère quy d'une part leur donne le relief et l'autorité nécessaire pour le bien de leurs devoirs avec plus d'honneur et de désintéressement."* Underneath this official verbiage, however, the real motive is but ill-disguised: the edict was only one of many schemes for raising funds for the army of the king. The office became thus hereditary and permanent, by right of purchase, in each bishopric or bailiwick of the *pays d'états*, and in the chief towns where sub-delegates already existed or where necessity seemed to demand their establishment. The sub-delegates were to receive all petitions addressed to the intendant and to forward them as soon as possible, with added information and advice. They were likewise to receive the orders of the intendant, to communicate them to the *maires*, *eschevins*, *conseils*, or *syndics* of their communities, and to see to the execution of them. They were to assist in the assessment and levy of the *taille* and other impositions, rendering to the intendant for this purpose an exact account of their parish visitations.† These offices were to be filled with "personnes capables que nous entre ceux de nos sujets quy nous seront présentés par les dits sieurs intendants et commis départy entre les mains desquels ils presteront le serment."

At a time when royalty was insisting upon the observance of court etiquette with the utmost rigor, it is no matter of surprise to find the intendants insisting punctiliously upon petty forms which they thought due to their social and political position, as bearers of royal mandate. Their anxious concern for matters of etiquette would have been ludicrous in an age less ardently devoted to formalities, but in the seventeenth century failure in the least punctilio was fatal to official influence and prestige. The

exercising his functions, other means were resorted to. When Beron at Rochelle fell ill and asked for a three months' leave of absence, the *contrôleur* assigned Pinon of Poitou to the vacancy. Pinon received a "gratification" of 3000 livres for these additional services. Boislisle, II. No. 486.

* Reprinted among *Pièces justificatives* in Boyer de Ste. Suzanne, p. 583.

† Boislisle, I. No. 1230, gives an interesting instruction given by an intendant to his sub-delegates "pour faire la visite des blés."

Correspondance administrative records more than a few petty wrangles over questions of precedence in the provincial estates. The intendant in Bretigny relates a quarrel that arose between himself and the First President over their respective positions in the opening procession of the assembly. The usage had always been for the intendant to be accompanied by the lieutenants general, while the two commissioners of the *conseil* preceded him, and the First President with the former president followed. In the absence of the lieutenants general, the First President claimed the right to accompany the intendant. The intendant protested vigorously and absolutely refused to suffer this presumption. Matters were smoothed over finally by the tact of M. le Maréchal de Châteaurenault, who had the intendant walk at his left.* The incident, trivial enough in itself, assumed great proportions in the eyes of the intendant, for he felt that his social and political prestige was at stake. Where there was a fair show of reason on the side of the intendants, the *conseil du roi* usually sustained their claims, justly feeling that it must secure respect for the personnel of the service. When an intendant of Auvergne felt himself aggrieved by certain imputations from the *présidial* of Clermont, that body received peremptory orders to go to the house of the intendant and to give him satisfaction "*en termes honnêtes.*"†

There can be no doubt that the intendants were socially ambitious, and nearly all show a disposition to magnify their office. Larcher, intendant in the town of Châlons, urged that the state purchase a house to serve as a fitting residence for the intendant. He supported his petition in this fashion: "Je ne sais si pareille chose s'est jamais pratiquée, mais l'on voit tous les jours faire de semblables impositions‡ pour les bureaux des trésoriers de France ou pour les logemens des élections ou autres compagnies, et l'on pourroit, ce me semble, à plus forte raison, en ordonner de mesme pour le logement d'un intendant, qui, en faisant les affaires du Roy, travaille aussy à celles de la généralité, et qui doit estre logé convenablement à son caractère, surtout dans une ville de passage telle que celle-cy, où il est souvent obligé de recevoir de grands

* Boislisle, II. No. 915. Another instance in Boislisle II. No. 1029. In this case the government did not approve of the pretensions of the intendant.
† Boislisle, I. No. 1891.
‡ He had suggested a general tax on the generality to defray the cost of the proposed mansion.

seigneurs et quelquefois des princes."* This last statement was
not overdrawn. It sometimes did fall to the lot of the intendants
to entertain members of the royal family, but with the worry and
expense which such visits seem to have entailed upon the intendant and the community, the honor was rather a doubtful one.†

Nothing is more hazardous than to attempt to estimate the
personal character of the intendants during the reign of Louis
XIV. Individual estimates are indeed possible, but sweeping
generalizations are inadmissible, so long as the official correspondence remains the prime source of authority. Contemporary
estimates are so palpably partisan that it would be folly to give
unreserved credence to either side. When the mayor and
consuls of Montauban wrote an ardent eulogy of the intendant,
and addressed it to the chancellor, he replied that nothing could
be more to the intendant's credit if all that they had said were
dictated by no other motive than fear of losing him, but he
added significantly, "comme tout ce que vous m'escrivés en sa
faveur n'est qu'une répétition de ce qui m'a esté escrit le mesme
jour de plusieurs endroits, il est à appréhender pour luy que ce
concert ne diminue beaucoup de la force de tous ces tesmoignages,
et qu'on ne les regarde comme des éloges visiblement mendiés."‡
Such instances warn against implicit confidence in "unsolicited"
testimonials even of the seventeenth century.

Evidence of corruption among the intendants is scanty.
Here and there an intendant was found implicated in fraud and
peculation, but such cases, if frequent, were effectually concealed.
Suspicions are aroused, it is true, when an intendant writes a
letter denying that he made 50,000 écus by issuing passports to
grain-dealers.§ He may have been honest,—the tone of the letter
indicates that he was,—but the opportunity for amassing private
fortunes in this way is apparent, and may have been secretly used
by some intendants. What creates a strong supposition in favor
of the general honesty of the intendants, is the fact that they kept
in such close contact with the *conseil*. Where a correspondence,
at once so minute and so comprehensive, is sustained between

---

* Boislisle, I. No. 1682.
† Foucault was domiciled in the château de Pau, "meublé des meubles de la
couronne," where his wife bore him a daughter, born, he records with pride, "dans le
lit où est né le roi Henri IV."—*Mémoires*, p. 93 and p. 108.
‡ Boislisle, II. Nos. 236 and 335.
‡ Depping, I. p. 954, No. 215.
§ Boislisle, I. No. 1253.

subordinate and superior, the possibility of undetected dishonesty is small indeed. There is almost no subject upon which the letters of the intendants to the ministers of state do not touch. So long as the ministry kept a firm hold upon the pulse of the intendants, irregularities of heart action were easily detected, for the service of the king demanded a whole-hearted devotion.*

* The *contrôleur* once wrote to Turgot at Tours. "La situation des affaires demande un homme tout entiers."—Boislisle, II. No. 489.

CHAPTER II.

Any attempt to find uniform regulations prescribing in detail the duties of the intendants, must prove futile, for the simple reason that none ever existed. Instructions covering special cases or even classes of cases are many, but general regulations there are none. The commission of each intendant was addressed directly to him and was never registered in Parlement. Moreover, these commissions not only varied between one intendant and another, but even altered their character as the intendant gave up one intendancy to assume another. Generalizations seem thus extremely hazardous at the very outset. But when all due allowance has been made for local variation, there still remain phases of the institution which are common to all intendants. In matters of finance, and particularly in the assessment and supervision of the *taille*, the functions of the intendants present greatest uniformity, but even in these cases the uniformity is more apparent than real. In the *pays d'états* the imposition and collection of the *taille* was entirely under the control of the estates or of commissioners appointed by them. The intendant might direct and supervise, but he might not control. In the *pays d'élection* the case was different, for, although originally the assessment of the *taille* was the work of elective officers,—the *élus*,—they had ceased to have any real independence, yielding to the intendants as royal agents.

The phraseology of the commission given to de Breteuil, intendant at Amiens, is, perhaps, typical of those addressed to intendants in the *pays d'élection.* "Vous faire répresenter les départemens des rolles de tailles et de l'impost du sel, vous transporter dans toutes les paroisses pour examiner et recognoistre sy lesdicts rolles ont esté bien et dubment faits suivant nos ordonnances et réglements, vous enquerir des sommes quy auront esté exigées par chacune année dans lesdictes paroisses pour frais d'huissiers et sergens et des concussions faites tant par eux que

par les receveurs et commis aux receptes, informer pareillement
des abus et malversations quy pourraient avoir esté faites dans
lesdits départmens des tailles............décerner toutes ordon
nances et viser toutes constraintes nécessaires pour le recouvre-
ment de nos dicts deniers, mesme faire compter par devant vous
tous les receveurs généraux et particuliers de nos finance et
autres quy ont eu le maniement de nos dicts deniers, assister et
présider au département d'iceux.............taxer d'office les
principaux habitans des paroisses quy se seraient fait décharger
trop modiquement par leur crédit et violence, et générallement
agir au regard des tailles selon et ainsy qu'il est porté par nos
ordonnances."*

The bare outline of such commissions was filled in by minute
instructions sent out yearly to all the intendants of the *pays
d'élection* by the *contrôleur général*. Special emphasis was laid
upon the visitations of the intendants in their departments, as a
necessary preliminary for determining the amount of the *taille*.
Certain injunctions repeat themselves year after year. The
intendant is urged to observe the resources of each election, the
taxes with which it is burdened, the condition of the tax-bearers,
the manner in which taxes are collected, the conduct of receivers,
abuses and the remedy for them, the condition of the farming
lands and of trade, and, in general, everything that will aid in
making up the annual list of the *taille.*† Upon the reports of
these annual visitations the *conseil des finances* relied in fixing
the *brevet de la taille,*‡ which was usually sent in July to the
treasurer and the intendant of each generality. Accompanying
this was an order to prepare the assessment. Treasurer and
intendant then submitted their report, and in September commissions were sent through the intendant to the treasurer, who, in
turn, passed them on to the officers of each election. Finally, in
October, the intendant and the treasurer went into each election,
and in the presence of the *élus* formally announced the amount to
be raised by the collectors.§

At first sight, the association of the treasurer with the intendants seems to imply almost a parity of power between them, but

* Boyer de Ste. Suzanne: *Pièces just.*, pp. 577 et seq.
† See among other letters, Boislisle, I. Nos. 274, 571; Colbert, II. p. 574.
‡ The expression might be loosely translated by the English term *budget*.
§ This procedure is indicated in Colbert, II. p. 83, No. 38; Colbert, II. p. 13 et te.
Depping, III. p. 233.

such a supposition is wide of the mark. The intendant possessed the determinative influence in the distribution of the burden of taxation between parish and parish, as the letters of Colbert prove beyond the shadow of a doubt.* It is to be noted, too, that while the local collectors assessed the individuals of each parish according to their own judgment, they were not so independent as might be inferred. They were constantly under the eye of the intendant or of his sub-delegates. Besides, the intendant possessed the reserved right to tax any person, or persons, whom the collector had passed over, or to augment the tax of those who had been unduly favored. This arbitrary power—*taxer d'office* —the intendant was repeatedly urged by the government to exercise "pour le soulagement des peuples."† Individuals thus taxed might, it is true, obtain relief through the *cour des aides*,‡ but an *arrêt du conseil* would effectively sustain the intendant and quash all decisions of other bodies.§ To dull the other edge of what might prove to be a double-edged weapon, the government forbade the intendant to use this power to *decrease* the taxation of any individual. ‖

Although the intendant was not allowed to diminish the amount of the *taille* on his own responsibility, he was expected to keep the government informed of losses which his province might have sustained through failure of crops or other cause, and to notify the government when a lightening of the tax burden seemed absolutely imperative. He was to take care to distribute the *taille* so as to relieve those districts which had suffered from reverses of any sort; the strong were to bear the burdens of the weak.¶ Aid to an unfortunate generality was not always bestowed by diminishing the *taille*. In many cases the king preferred to send money to the sufferers; and the intendant then became the dispenser of the royal charities,—charities, it should be said, which were numerous and for the most part wisely directed.° In one instance the king sent to an intendant 20,000 livres to be distributed in a parish that had been ravaged by a hail storm, but with this sagacious warning: "Il faut bien prendre garde de ne pas mettre

* Depping, III. p. 34.
† Colbert, II. p. 148, No. 97; also p. 151, No. 108.
‡ One of the numerous administrative courts.
§ A good example of this in Colbert, II. p. 212, No. 177.
‖ Colbert, II. p. 266, No. 232.
¶ Boislisle, I. No. 461.
° Boislisle, I. Nos. 227, 378, 692, 937.

les peuples sur le pied de recevoir ainsy des diminutions et gratifications toutes les fois qu'il tombera quelque gresle. Ces sortes
de secours extraordinaires, que S. M. ne refuse jamais dans
les besoins pressans, ne doivent pas s'appliquer à beaucoup
d'occasions, dans lesquelles il souffroit bien souvent d'user de
ménagement et d'apporter un peu plus d'application qu'à l'ordinaire, pour exciter le travail et l'industrie des contribuables."[*]

Thrown sometimes upon his own resources, the intendant
had to provide for the poor of certain parishes by appealing to
the well-to-do classes for voluntary charities. And when such
appeals met with no response, he did not hesitate to employ more
drastic means. Chauvelin at Amiens threatened to quarter poor
families upon certain affluent individuals whose purses did not
open readily, and he was as good as his word; he housed several
families in this fashion, with results so gratifying that he hastened
to recount his praiseworthy deeds to the appreciative *contrôleur*.[†]

Collectors of taxes were chosen by the inhabitants of each
parish and were made personally responsible for the sums to be
raised. If for any reason they were unable to collect the amount
assessed, they might be imprisoned at the solicitation of the
receivers. This fate befell many an unlucky collector. In Tours
so many collectors were imprisoned that Colbert wrote a sharp
letter to the intendant, bidding him to inquire into this lamentable
state of things.[‡] Inquiries brought to light an iniquitous practice,
which was probably not confined to a single generality. It
seems that certain shrewd individuals in a community would
sometimes secure the election of a collector who they felt
reasonably sure would be willing to go to prison for insolvency,
if he and his family were sufficiently remunerated. It was far
more economical to support an insolvent collector in prison than
it was to pay the *taille*. Such practices were hard to root out, and
the intendant often found himself utterly unable to reach the
guilty parties. Moreover, the collectors themselves were often
guilty of petty fraud, receiving *gratifications*, for example, for
partially remitting the taxes of unscrupulous individuals.

With imprisonment menacing them in default of payment,
it is not strange that collectors resorted to every means in their

* Boislisle, I. No. 468.
† Boislisle, I. No. 1174.
‡ Colbert, II. p. 71, No. 19.

power to extort money, or its equivalent, from the tax-payers. A royal ordinance forbade the seizure of beasts of burden for non-payment of the *taille*, but the rule seems to have been honored more in the breach than in the observance. Colbert explained the situation by saying that the king desired to check the arbitrary seizure of live stock by collectors, without depriving them, however, of the power to use this means as a last resort.* This left to the intendants the delicate, and rather dubious, task of deciding when an ordinance of His Majesty should be deliberately transgressed.

Custom permitted the use of *huissiers* and *sergens* by collectors to force payments, but they resorted not infrequently to the still more dreaded *porteurs de constraintes* and to *logements effectifs*.† This latter practice was discouraged by the king, although it was not absolutely forbidden. "Vous devez travailler par tous les moyens possibles à retrancher la constrainte par logement effectif dans l'estendue de vostre généralité.............. Travaillez à l'oster pour restablir la constrainte par voye d'huissier, s'il est possible."‡ But the course of the government was far from consistent. Instances abound where, at the urgent request of an intendant, the government sanctioned the use of the soldiery to secure payments of the *taille*. To the intendant at Bourges, Colbert wrote in 1662: "J'ai écrit un billet à M. le Marquis de Louvois pour l'expédition des ordres que vous avez demandés, afin de loger des troupes dans les paroisses de vostre généralité qui refusent de payer la taille suivant le rôle que vous en avez envoyé, de sorte que je crois que si vous ne les avez pas encore reçus vous les recevrez incessamment."§ On the back of a similar petition from the intendant at Limoges in 1708 the *contrôleur* wrote: "Lui écrire de ménager les constraintes avec prudence. Avertir, avant que d'envoyer les soldats, qu'on ait à payer dans un terme certain; si non, qu'au jour marqué ils seront logés dans les maisons de ceux qui refusent de payer."‖ It is well to bear

---

*Colbert, II. p. 168, No. 121.

† It is difficult to find English equivalents for these terms. *Huissiers* and *sergens* might possibly be rendered by the terms *bailiff* and *constable;* both were officers associated with judicial tribunals. For *porteur de constraintes,* the term *sheriff* would be a fair equivalent. The expression *logements effectifs* refers to the practice, explained below, of quartering soldiers to intimidate obstinate tax-bearers.

‡ Colbert, II. p. 224, No. 189.

§ Colbert, II. p. 234, No. 201.

‖ Boislisle, II. No. 1371 note. Other instances in Boislisle, I. Nos. 176, 706, 1623; also II. Nos. 781, 1252.

these instances in mind in discussing the "unparalleled" treatment of the Protestants by *logements effectifs*.

Quite as instructive is the part which the intendant played in the *pays d'états* in securing from the estates the grant of the *don gratuit*. The intendant and the governor, or the lieutenant-governor, were usually the representatives of the crown in these provincial assemblies. As the titular representative of the royal power, the governor formally opened the session, but he rarely appeared in the assembly thereafter. When the deliberations actually began, it was the intendant who presented the demands or wishes of the crown, and stated the amount of the *don gratuit* that was expected. It was the intendant, too, rather than the governor, upon whom the government relied to persuade the assembly to yield to the royal demands. In the earlier part of the reign of Louis XIV., at least, the provincial estates had not been reduced to that spirit of servile obedience which they showed in the eighteenth century. The *don gratuit* had long since lost its original meaning, to be sure, but the form of voluntary gift was preserved and the amount desired by the crown was secured only with the greatest difficulty.

It was customary for the commissioners to demand a sum considerably larger than that which they were secretly authorized to take, while the estates would at first vote a much smaller sum, only to agree, in most cases, upon the sum which the commissioners were bidden to accept.* The tactics of the intendant would do credit to a modern politician at a political convention. It was thought to be of considerable importance that the archbishop chosen to preside over the assembly should be one well-disposed to the king. In this matter the knowledge of the intendant stood the government in good stead, for if his influence was not great enough to secure the choice of his favorite, he could at least put the court in possession of information that would bring about the desired result. Sundry letters to the bishops of the province would leave them in no doubt as to the choice of the king, and woe betide them if they ventured to cross the will of His Majesty!†

Since it was of greater importance to secure the subserviency of the deputies, the intendant left no stone unturned "pour

* See Depping, I. *passim.*
† Depping, I. p. 82, No. 23.

mesnager les esprits et les eschauffer." On occasions he resorted
unblushingly to downright bribery. Wrote one intendant: "Si
vous voulez que pour faciliter les affaires du roi l'on y fasse
quelque dépense, mandez-le-moi, s'il vous plaist, pour prendre ses
mesures de bonne heure." On the margin of this note Colbert
wrote in assent, "Quelque dépense."* Even after the session
had begun, the intendant continued to make his influence felt.
In the general assembly† of Provence, the deputies were wont
to deliberate for several days behind closed doors, to the exclu-
sion of the royal commissioners. These secret sessions were
extremely objectionable to the intendant Lebret. He and the
Archbishop of Aix put their heads together and finally decided
to take a bold stand against the practice. Next year the intendant
resolutely kept his seat, when the time came for him to withdraw,
and the estates, taken by surprise, voted, without a dissenting
voice, the 600,000 livres demanded by the king.‡ The presence
of the intendant, the delegated emissary of the king, in these
provincial assemblies, was undoubtedly a potent cause for their
becoming facile and harmless instruments of the central government.§ The reflection that this outwardly unassuming officer
was watching with lynx-eyed sharpness his every move, and
noting his most casual words, quickened more than one indifferent
deputy into at least ostensible zeal for the service of the king.‖

It is a mistake to suppose that in these earlier years of the
reign the governor was a mere figure-head, but it is true that the
balance of power in the *pays d'états* was steadily gravitating
to the intendant.¶ Although the governor and intendant act
together as royal commissioners, and address joint reports to
the *contrôleur*, it is evident that greater reliance is placed upon

---

* Depping, I. p. 51, No. 5.
Another intendant wrote.:"Nous avons esté obligés de vous servir du secours que
vous avez trouvé bon que l'on prist pour faciliter l'affaire du roy: je vous en envoiroy
le detail par le premier ordinaire, et les noms de ceux qui ont receu ces gratifications."—
Depping, I. p. 123, No. 46.

† The *États provinciaux* of Provence had given way to a less independent assembly
called the *assemblée générale*.

‡ Marchand. p. 98. A similar practice was in vogue in the estates of Languedoc:
Monin, p. 131.

§ See the testimony of the Bishop of Marseille: Depping, I. p. 405.

‖ Depping, I. p. 217, No. 101, gives a *mémoire* on the conduct of an assembly submitted by one intendant to Colbert: "M. de Viviers a faict tout ce qui dépendait de luy,
avec zèle et affection. M. de Saint-Pons a toujours esté opposé a tout............ M. de
Polignac, bien. M. de Rabat, M. de Gouges, M. de Saint-Sulpice, *idem.*"
M. de Saint-Pons was forbidden by letter from the King to attend the next
assembly.

¶ See the admirable discussion of the position of the governor in Marchand, Chapter II.

the intendant, who by the very nature of his office is better informed on local administrative affairs. Immediately after the intendant and his colleague had submitted their joint report, the intendant would frequently address a private missive to the *contrôleur*, relating, confidentially, this or that aspect of the political situation. "J'ai fait voir au Roy particulièrement," wrote Colbert to the intendant at Toulouse, "le mémoire secret que vous m'avez envoyé, concernant la diversité des avis qui ont esté portés à la dernière déliberation, et Sa Majesté a fort bien remarqué ceux qui se sont distingués par leur zèle à contribuer à sa satisfaction, et les autres qui s'en sont éloignés en opinant autrement; et vous ne devez pas craindre que je vous commettre en rien, ni en cela, ni en toutes les autres choses que vous me manderez en confidence."* On the reverse side of scores of letters addressed to the *contrôleur général* by the governor and the lieutenant-governor of Provence, were written in the hand of the *contrôleur* such significant memoranda as these: "Se concerter avec M. Lebret;" "Savoir la vérité de M. Lebret."†

An important financial mission forced upon the intendants was that of supervising the finances of the towns and smaller communities. The commission to de Breteuil, who was made intendant at Amiens, read: "Verifier les dettes des communautéz jugez de la validité d'icelles ensemble les procès pour raison desdicts debtes et de leurs cautions et co-obligés dont elles sont garantés et leur accorder les délais et les tolérances que vous estimerez nécessaires vous faire réprésenter les comptes de ceux quy ont en maniement des denrées communs et d'octrois desdictes villes ensemble les pièces justificatives d'iceux vous en attribuent à cette fin toute jurisdiction et connaissance sauf l'appel en nostre conseil d'icelle.‡ The reports of the intendants reveal an almost unparalleled history of corruption and maladministration in these communities. Bouchu reported three small towns in his generality, which together had an indebtedness of 1,500,000 livres. The disasters of war had caused part of this, but the corrupt administration of the last quarter of a century was largely responsible for it. *Maires* and *échevins* would fix the amount to

* Colbert, IV. p. 41, No. 26. This letter accompanied the report of the royal commissioners.
† Marchand, p. 75.
‡ Boyer de Ste. Suzanne, *Pièces just.*, p. 578.

be raised far above the immediate municipal needs, and then either coolly pocket the surplus, or expend it in celebrations and festivities.* Towns often squandered large amounts in endless litigations and in useless expenses of one sort and another.†

It was this chronic state of disorder that the government undertook to remedy. One of the first cares of Colbert was to rid the communities of their indebtedness, "cette vermine qui les ronge continuellement." Again and again, in letters to each and all, he urges the intendants to effect the liquidation of the debts of the towns.‡ The task was a heavy one, as the *contrôleur* himself admitted,§ and more than one intendant found himself helpless before the rings and the bosses of these unhappy communities. When the intendant addressed himself to his task and summoned the inhabitants of a village to assign to their creditors, he would often meet with no response except from the poorer people, who were totally ignorant of public affairs; the really responsible parties would simply ignore the summons.‖ In the larger towns the opposition was scarcely less effective, though it was, perhaps, less open. Summoned to present their accounts, the town officials would resort to the most exasperating subterfuges and delays. Under these circumstances, it is not surprising to find this work of the intendants protracted through a long series of years.

Colbert was soon persuaded that all these efforts would be only palliatives, if no measures were taken to prevent the communities from incurring new obligations and relapsing into their previous condition. A few months of misfortune, or maladministration, sufficed in most cases to plunge small communities into their former helplessness. In 1680 Colbert requested an expression of opinion from the intendants in regard to measures best adapted to meet these exigencies.¶ The intendants

---

* Depping, I. p. 606, No. 30.

† Depping, I. p. 859, No. 110.
  Boislisle, I. Nos. 1812, 476.

‡ In 1670 Colbert wrote, in a circular letter to the intendants, "La liquidation des dettes des communautés estant importante au point que vous le sçavez pour le soulagement des peuples, il n'y a rien a quoy vous deviez donner plus de soin et d'application qu'à la conclusion de cette affaire."—Colbert, IV. p. 50, No. 35.

§ "Je sçais bien que ce travail n'est pas un travail d'un jour, mais j'estime que si vous le commencez avec ordre, et que, sans embrasser toute la généralité, vous vous contentiez de travailler à une seule élection et que vous y donniez toute l'application nécessaire, vous aurez la satisfaction de voir avancer ce travail beaucoup plus mesme que vous ne le croyez."—Colbert, IV. p. 146, No. 141.

‖ For a graphic description of the difficulties that one intendant encountered, see Depping, I. p. 758, No. 67.

¶ Colbert, IV. p. 138, No. 133.

responded, each with his own project, but three years slipped away before the government adopted a workable scheme.

The details of the plan finally adopted have a right to a place in these pages only in so far as they bring to mind the burden of accumulated cares which the intendant bore. In the first place, the system provided that town officials should submit to the intendant of the generality a statement of the town revenues and of the leases [*baux*] made during the previous ten years, together with all town reports which had hitherto been made. With these official records as a basis, the current expenses of the town, up to a certain amount, were to be fixed by the intendant; beyond that amount, by the *conseil du roi*. These current expenditures were to be met by the *revenues patrimoniaux,* or, if these sources of revenue were wanting, by such ways and means as the inhabitants should determine upon in assembly. The result of these deliberations, with the intendant's advice, was then to be submitted to the *conseil* for approval or disapproval. All sales, loans, and alienations of property and of *octrois*, were forbidden except in three cases; i. e., for the lodging of troops, for the re-building of the naves of churches that had collapsed, and for relief in time of pestilence. In these instances the people might meet in assembly, and by a majority vote authorize the negotiation of a loan, at the same time deciding how the loan should eventually be paid. This action was then to be reported to the intendant, who might approve it and authorize the loan. He was then in turn to notify the *conseil*, in order that it might act upon the ways and means proposed to repay the loan. The moneys loaned were to be lodged in the hands of a receiver, or of one of the prominent citizens, who, in the presence of the intendant, was to render to the *maire* and *échevins*, or to the assembled community, an exact account of his disbursements. Creditors were forbidden to bring action against public officials, even for the recovery of legitimate loans, except by written order of the intendant. Communities and public officials were forbidden to begin any suit at law, or to send a deputation of citizens to the royal court, without the consent of the people given in assembly, and approved by the intendant. The duration and the expenses of such "deputations" were also to be regulated by the

*The expression is capable of various interpretations. What is meant is probably the public lands or estates which yielded a revenue in the form of rent.

intendant.* Re-affirmations of this edict in succeeding years†
indicate how difficult it was for even the watchful intendants
to bring order into the financial chaos of the communities.
Deputations to the court continued to be a fruitful source of
expense, even when honestly conducted, since they too often
served no other purpose than to satisfy the greed of certain
leaders of the ring that controlled local politics.‡ The royal
ministers did everything in their power to check this practice.
Colbert was most emphatic in his instructions on this point, since
he rightly held that nothing contributed more to the financial
ruin of communities. As a warning against future deputations,
he told one intendant that he had kept a deputy from Marseille
awaiting an audience three weeks!§

Few tasks are more baffling than that of attempting to define
precisely the functions of the intendant in the administration of
justice. The picture which France of the seventeenth century
presents, with its bewildering array of *justices royales, justices
ecclésiastiques, justices seigneuriales,* and even *justices munici-
pales,* is hazy at best, but it loses nearly all its distinct outlines
when the peculiar relation of the intendants to the established
courts is brought into the field of vision, for it must be remem-
bered that no edict ever created the office, or exactly defined its
competence. Nevertheless, the task is not a hopeless one. Two
sources remain from which valuable information may be drawn:
the commissions and the instructions of the intendants. Lament-
ably brief and woefully contradictory though they be, these
documents may be made to yield valuable facts, if they are constantly compared with the reports of the intendants; but, after
all, the surest course is to follow the intendant himself in his
labors, now here and now there.

True to the general nature of his office, the intendant
possessed, first and foremost, general supervisory and regulative
power over the courts of justice and over their personnel. The

---

* Isambert. XIX. No. 1055.
† It was re-issued in part in 1687 and 1703: Isambert. XX. Nos. 1283 and 1866.
‡ Two astute politicians from Provence, who were sent on a deputation to Paris to
conduct a lawsuit, spent some 12,000 livres on their own account and reckoned in that
sum as part of their legitimate expenses. The intendant, however, was equal to the
occasion and obliged them to make restitution: Boislisle, I. p. 476.
§ Colbert, IV. p. 164, No. 163.

commission of Breteuil read: "Informer de tous les abbus quy se commettent en l'administration de la justice, soit en matières civiles par la longueur et la multiplicité de procédures inutiles .... comme aussy des abbus quy se rencontrent aux frais de la police, de tous les crimes qui resteront impunis, des raisons et fauteurs de cette impunité, exciter mesme et provoquer sur ce sujet suivant nos ordonnances les plaintes de ceux quy, par quelque considération que ce soit, n'ont osé et n'ont pu se plaindre jusqu'à présent, informer d'office et décréter contre ceux quy se trouveront coupables et contre lesquels les juges ordinaires des lieux ne procéderaient pas selon le debvoir de leur charges et envoier vos informations et décrets en nostre conseil."[*] Furthermore, the intendant was enjoined to inspect the *procès-verbaux* of the *prévosts*, of the *maréchaux*,[†] and of other inferior courts, and also to review the officers of the court to see if they are properly equipped and armed, "comme ils doibvent estre pour le bien de nostre service." To follow the intendant into all the varied activities which this comprehensive duty of supervision and control inspired, would be a most remunerative study, but for present purposes a mere sketch must suffice.

Soon after entering upon his duties as *contrôleur général* and leading counselor of the king, Colbert saw the need of reform in the administration of justice. It was probably a first step in this direction when he summoned the intendants to prepare careful notes on the personnel of the various courts in their generalities.[‡] It was a delicate undertaking. How well the work was done, it is impossible to say. There is reason to suspect that the personal equation often entered largely into these estimates of character and efficiency; but the persistent frequency with which such expressions as *"interéssé," "de peu de conscience," "aimé ses intérests,"* repeat themselves, indicates a sorry state of things in the provinces and the necessity of a sharp

---

[*] Boyer de Ste. Suzanne, *Pièces justificatives*, p. 581.

The commission to Lebret is more concise: "Procéder au règlement et réformation de la justice selon nos ordonnances, reconnaître si nos officiers font leur devoir en l'exercise et fonction de leurs charges, ouïr les plaintes et doléances de nos sujets, pourvoir ou faire pourvoir sur icelles par les officiers établis sur les lieux ou autres que vous aviserez, ordonner aux procureurs dudit pays, consuls des villes et aux prévôts des maréchaux, leurs lieutenants greffiers et archers et autres nos justiciers, ce que vous verrez être du bien de ladite province et de notre service." Marchand, *Pièces justificatives*, p. 362.

[†] These courts formed a part of the *justice seigneuriale du roi*, and took cognizance of those cases, which, in earlier times, had belonged to the *connétable* of France, as head of the military tribunals.

[‡] "Notes secrètes sur le personnel de tous les Parlements et cours des comptes du royaume."—Depping, II. p. 33.

watch over the judiciary. Eternal vigilance was here the price
of simple justice. Charges of corruption are too frequent
throughout the reign to permit any doubt as to the venality of
the courts. "Je suis après à faire le procès aux juges de village,
qui ruinent les peuples par la grande authorité qu'ils se donnent,
et qui traitent de tous les crimes à prix d'argent,"* wrote de
Berulle from Auvergne. Somewhat later, this same intendant
closed an account of the corrupt practices in the courts with the
pithy comment, "Enfin tout pille en ce pays!"

The formulation of the Ordinance of 1667,—the *Code Louis*,
as it came to be called,—was another step forward in the reform
of the administration of justice.† Its purpose is indicated in the
preamble, where reform of the procedure of the courts in the
interest of despatch and uniformity is emphasized.‡ Obvious
as the need of such reform was, the ordinance met with resolute
opposition from many of the parlements; that of Pau resisted
with exasperating obstinacy for nearly a score of years.§ Again
the government had to rely on the intendants, and again they
proved themselves equal to the occasion.

By virtue of his commission the intendant was empowered to
form a special tribunal and pass judgment in last resort upon
certain cases, with appeal only to the *conseil*; in a certain sense,
he was himself part of the judicial machinery of the government.
Although the form of the commissions varied, the competence of
the intendants was substantially the same. The language of one
commission was: "Voulant que des cas susdites‖ et des contraven-
tions à nos ordonnances, exactions, excès, violences, assassinats,
et autres crimes, même des rebellions et autres oppositions ou
empêchements qui pourraient être apportés directement ou indi-
rectement à la levée de nos droit, soit par nos sujets de ladite
province et terres adjacentes, soit par lesdits gens de guerre vous
avez à faire et parfaire le procès aux coupables jusques à juge-

---

* Boislisle, I. No. 245.
  Foucault reported from Béarn: "Les officiers du Parlement sont peu instruits
et mal intentionnés pour la justice. Ils ont peu de soumission aux ordres du Roy et
du conseil. Il n'y a aucune règle dans la forme de rendre les jugements, les officiers
demeurent souvent juges dans leur propre cause ou de leurs parens."—Boislisle, I.
No. 47.
  † Chéruel, II. p. 263 et seq.
  ‡ Isambert, XVIII. p. 103.
  §The struggle of Foucault with this refractory *parlement* forms an interesting
chapter in the history of his intendancy: *Mémoires de Foucault*, p. 110.
  That is: "désordres," "menées secretes," "tous ports d'armes," "assemblées
illicites," "levées des gens de guerre sans commissions," "tous délits, violences et excès."

ment définitif et exécution d'icelui inclusivement sans appel et en dernier ressort."* The intendant was obliged to associate with him "des juges ou gradués† au nombre porté par nos ordonnances;" but by the terms of his commission, he was bidden, whenever he deemed necessary, "seoir et présider en tous sièges royaux de ladite province et autres jurisdictions d'icelle," and it is often impossible to determine from the official correspondence whether the intendant is sitting in judgment with associates in a special court, or in some one of the *présidiaux*. It is probable that so long as he could accomplish what he desired through the channels of ordinary justice, the intendant forebore to constitute himself a special tribunal. The necessity of choosing associate judges seems, at first sight, to have been a serious limitation to the jurisdiction of the intendant, since all decisions were given by majority vote; but inasmuch as he was free to choose whom he liked, he could nearly always be sure of the pliancy of his appointees.‡ In point of fact, the intendant's voice was usually determinative. It would have required judges of more than ordinary stamina to thwart what was tacitly accepted as the will of the king, pronounced through his own agent and representative.

Besides this jurisdiction, civil and criminal, in affairs of *la justice ordinaire*, the intendant possessed other important duties. Attention has already been called to the jurisdiction which the intendant exercised in suits at law arising from *"impositions aux taxes d'office"* in the *pays d'élection*. When the capitation§ was established in 1695, a royal declaration gave entire jurisdiction over contested cases to the intendant.‖ Litigations arising from the building of highways and bridges and other public works, also fell within the competence of the intendant.

It was almost inevitable that the intendant should become involved in continual wrangles with the ordinary courts of justice. Such powers as have been described created the possibility of arbitrary interference in the course of justice; and the

---

*Marchand, *Pièces just.*, p. 363.
† The term *gradués* was applied to those who had gained the title of *docteur en droit*.
‡ Marchand, p. 476.
§ A personal tax not unlike our poll-tax.
‖ For a careful statement of this phase of the intendant's duties, which lies beyond the scope of the present study, the reader is referred to Dareste, *"La justice administrative,"* pp. 119 et seq.

intendant was not slow in taking advantage of his opportunities; often, no doubt, out of mere officiousness or mistaken zeal for the service of his royal master. Such interference, it goes without saying, would have been subversive of the established courts, if it had been capriciously continued. Again and again the ministry saw itself obliged to caution meddlesome intendants to avoid any encroachment upon the competence of the ordinary courts.*

That which transformed the *intendant de justice* from a mere judicial functionary with powers of supervision, and made of him a puissant, royal commissioner in matters of justice, was the practice of removing, or evoking, cases from the ordinary courts and of giving the intendants cognizance of them by an *arrêt d'attribution*. Nothing contributed more to extend the royal power in the provinces and to destroy the vestiges of independence which the local courts still possessed.† The claim had long been recognized, that suits in which the crown had an interest might be evoked from the ordinary courts of justice and transferred to specially designated tribunals. By the very slightest extension of these pretensions what cases might not be withdrawn from the ordinary courts! If the course of justice was perverted by corrupt judges or obstructed by indifferent ones, an *arrêt du conseil* would put any cases within the competence of the intendant; or, if the royal ordinances were balked by the spirit of particularism that still came to the surface now and then, an *arrêt du conseil* would leave the intendant undisputed master of the situation. The absolutism of Louis XIV. preferred silently to undermine opposition, but there were times when it marched ruthlessly to its goal.

---

* Colbert. VI. p. 30, No. 1².
† De Tocqueville. *L'Ancien Régime*, chap. IV.

CHAPTER III.

THE POLICE DUTIES OF THE INTENDANT.

If the charges given to the intendant had been simply financial and judicial, they would have made him an officer with wide-reaching powers, but when those attributes summed up in the phrase *intendant de police* were given to him, the intendant became possessed of vast authority. The modern concept of the police power, as the power to watch for and prevent infractions upon the legitimate sphere of individual autonomy, is none too clear; in the seventeenth century no distinctions at all were drawn. The police power was confounded with the entire internal administration of the government.* The tendency of the crown was to absorb all governmental functions and to reduce individual initiative and local autonomy to lowest terms. This self-imposed task of absorption and restriction made imperative the development of a most exacting system of supervision and control, and this system was confided to the intendants. In its broadest extension the police power of these officers fairly enveloped the internal administrative apparatus of the government.

It should be remarked at the outset that the very nature of the duty of surveillance and control confers great discretionary powers. Where the royal power assumes all governmental functions, it must, perforce, act through agents who will be its eyes and ears. Upon them it must rely for intimate knowledge of local affairs and for summary action in exigencies that arise. There must come times when the whole weight of royal power must be vested in these agents, to be wielded at their discretion. Such circumstances made of the intendant a veritable king, ruling by delegated right. It was these considerations that impressed Law, when he made the often-quoted remark: "Sachez que ce royaume de France est gouverné par trente intendants. Vous n'avez ni parlements, ni états, ni gouverneurs;

* Burgess, Comparative Constitutional Law, I. pp. 214, 215.

ce sont trente maîtres des requêtes commis aux provinces de qui dépendent le malheur ou le bonheur de ces provinces, leur abondance, ou leur stérilité."

Nearly all commissions agree in according to the intendants the task of maintaining the public peace, in so far as it should be threatened by the soldiers in garrison in their generalities, or by any riotous subjects of the king. The charge was usually given in such language as this: "Aussi vous vous enquerrez du déportement et façon de vivre des gens de guerre, qui sont ou seront ci-après en garnison dans les villes et places dudit pays, et si l'ordre par nous établi pour le payement de leur solde, vivres, routes, et logement est entièrement gardé et observé, vous employant à ce qu'ils soient contenus sous la discipline militaire et ne se licencient en rien à la foule et oppression de nos sujets."* Although this particular duty dated back undoubtedly to the earliest days of the institution, it had by no means become a mere formality. The succession of edicts and ordinances emanating from the *conseil*, to restrain the license of the soldiery, attest the lawlessness of the times and the necessity for these injunctions to the intendants.† The reports of the intendants are full of tales of lawless deeds committed by the regular army as well as by the militia.‡

In the exercise of this, as in so many of his duties, the intendant was brought face to face with other officers, within whose competence the matters properly belonged which were confided to him in this general way. Military discipline belonged of right to the commanders of the army, or to courts martial; the intendant might not interfere. It was only when friction of any sort arose between soldier and civilian, that the intendant assumed jurisdiction; but here again was the possibility of conflict, if the intendant intrenched too far upon the disciplinary powers of the commandants. The wise course, and that which the intendant usually and tactfully adopted, was to suffer the military authority to precede his own, and to act only in default of action by the military tribunals.§ The competence of the intendant when

---

* Lebret's commission in Provence, from Marchand, p. 362.

† Isambert, XVIII. Nos. 530, 531, 535; also XIX. No. 694, and XX. No. 1944.

‡ "J'ajouteray encore," wrote the intendant of Moulins, "avec vostre permission, que rien ne ruine plus le plat pays que cette milice; ils font des concussions, des violences, plus que toutes les autres troupes réglées." Boislisle, I. No. 1428; see also Boislisle, I. No. 1158.

§ Dareste, *La justice administrative en France*, pp. 132, 133. The chapter on the

constituting an extraordinary tribunal, has already been noted. Its decisions were summary and forceful; the culprit rarely escaped judgment, and punishment was speedy and sure. In the memoirs of Foucault there is this significant item: "J'ai condamné deux dragons du regiment de Tessé à être pendus, pour avoir tué un consul et un habitant de Beaumont qui avoient voulu [les empêcher de] violer la femme de leur hôte."* Again, "Les troupes ont fait beaucoup de désordres dans leurs quartiers, cette année .... et j'ai été obligé de punir plusieurs officiers et de faire pendre des cavaliers, dragons, et soldats."† The thorough-going character of Foucault's administration of justice is evidenced by a letter from Louvois, in which the intendant was warned not to cut off the noses of deserters too short, since the complete loss of that valuable member made the victim unfit for service on the galleys.‡

Much the same policy was followed by the intendant in the suppression of riots, and other public disturbances of a more serious type. When the course of ordinary justice failed, or when the ordinary officers for the maintenance of the public peace were unable to cope with the disorders, then the intendant made the weight of his influence felt. At his beck and call was the entire police force of the generality, for by virtue of his commission he might summon the maréchausée,§ or even the regular troops, to assist him in the preservation of law and order. The intendant was rarely obliged to resort to this last measure, for the mere threat usually sufficed to sober the hot-heads. An intendant at Moulins has left an unusually graphic account of a riot that occurred in his generality, and of the way in which it was suppressed. A rumor that the gabelle was to be established in the town of Aubusson had thrown the people into despair. In their rage the women pillaged one of the depôts of salt, and a riotous demonstration ensued. The arrival of the intendant on the scene and his threat to summon a regiment of dragoons brought the rabble to their senses. In the presence of the royal

judicial functions of the intendants is admirable, although much is applicable to the intendants of the eighteenth century rather than to those of the seventeenth century.
* *Mémoires de Foucault*, p. 32.
† *Mémoires de Foucault*, p. 36.
‡ *Mémoires de Foucault*, p. 151. Loss of nose and condemnation to galley-service was the punishment for desertion prescribed by ordinance.
§ Mounted police.

agent they seemed to realize for the first time the enormity of
their offence and the probable consequences of it. As the
intendant passed through the streets, men and women threw
themselves at his feet, begging for mercy, like repentant children.
With a mixture of paternal kindness and official severity, the
intendant succeeded in restoring order and in persuading the
people to restore the depot which they had destroyed in such
rebellious fashion.*

Object of special solicitude to the intendants was the *gabelle*
and the abuses and disorders which that pernicious institution
entailed. The term had come to be applied solely to the excise
duties on salt, which were farmed out on conditions that varied
greatly in different parts of the realm.† Usually the farmers of
the *gabelle* paid a fixed sum to the king and thereby acquired the
right to exploit his subjects. Where special tribunals [*greniers
à sel*] took cognizance of all infractions of the ordinances and had
a constabulary force to secure respect for the law, the intendant's
duties were largely the familiar one of surveillance. He had to
see to it, on the one hand, that the people were not victimized
by the rapacity of the farmers of the *gabelle*, and, on the other
hand, that the latter were not defrauded by the all too prevalent
practice of smuggling salt from the more favored districts into
those where the *gabelle* rested with crushing weight upon the
people.

In many parts of France a contraband trade in salt was
carried on with almost no attempt at concealment. Near Amiens
an organized band of forty desperadoes, who styled themselves
"la bande royale," pursued their illicit trade with the greatest
audacity.‡ The intendant who reported this state of things
declared that half of the *gardes des gabelles*§ were bribed and

---

* Boislisle, II. No. 595. For a similar instance see Boislisle, II. No. 703.
† See Cheruel, *Dictionnaire hist. des institutions, etc.*, article *gabelle*; also Rambaud.
Hist. de la civilisation française, pp. 160, 161; also Dareste, *Hist. de l'admin. en France*,
pp. 101-103. France was divided into five distinct districts: the *pays de grandes gabelles*,
in which the excise was assessed very much like the *taille*, or in which freedom of purchase was permitted with a minimum fixed by law for each person and for each family;
the *pays de petites gabelles*; the *pays de salines*, where the excise was levied with reference to the marshes from which salt was obtained; the *pays rédimés*, where the people
were forced to buy at a fixed price of authorized merchants; the *pays exempts*, where
the conditions were similar to those in the *pays rédimés*.
‡ Boislisle, I. No. 115.
§ Special constables or police officers, in the pay of the farmers of the *gabelle*.

themselves engaged in smuggling. In some districts the soldiers made common cause with the smugglers, and offered open resistance to the *gardes*. The intendant of Berry reported a pitched battle between the *gardes* and a mixed band of smugglers and cavaliers. The latter made good their retreat, but only with the loss of several of their number.[*] Such incidents were by no means isolated.[†] In Champagne the *gardes* were practically powerless before the bands of dragoons and cavaliers, so that the intendant appealed to the king to forbid the commanders of troops to allow their men to leave their rooms at night. The commanders, he maintained, were responsible for these disorders, inasmuch as they granted leave of absence to their men in order to profit by the pay which was thus forfeited.[‡]

Auvergne was one of the *pays rédimés* and enjoyed in consequence a relative degree of freedom from the hated excise on salt, but as it bordered upon *pays de grandes gabelles*, its frontiers were infested with smugglers. Since public opinion countenanced the traffic, and even gentlemen of position participated in it, the intendant was well nigh powerless. The magistrates of the *présidial*, he declared, were "sous le coup de la terreur;" prisoners easily escaped the clutches of the law by liberal bribes; processes carried on appeal to the *cours des aides* were ineffectual. For two years nothing had been done to repress the disorders.[§] In spite of this discouraging outlook, the intendant began a series of energetic measures. Stationing four companies of dragoons in the border parishes, he had the *gardes* deployed in brigades near by, so that they might be in communication with his troops and might be detected if they connived at any smuggling. Menaced by the irate inhabitants, these brigades had to withdraw temporarily, but, nothing daunted, the intendant remanded them to their post and publicly declared, that if any harm were done to them, the village would be held responsible and would be burned. In a single village four people were hanged, and ten condemned to the galleys for smuggling.[‖] And when even this ruthless severity did not suffice to intimidate

* Boislisle, I. No. 112.
† See also Boislisle, II. No. 668.
‡ Boislisle, I. No. 183.
§ Boislisle, II. No. 729.
‖ In all probability the intendant was acting under authority of *arrêts du conseil*. See Boislisle, II. No. 729.
Boislisle, II. No. 755.

the obstinate village folk, he summoned them to a public
assembly and forbade any, on pain of being prosecuted as a
smuggler, to leave the parish for more than two days, without a
certificate from the parish priest. Twice a week a sub-delegate
was to call the roll of the inhabitants to catch any delinquents.

In Languedoc, which, with Provence, formed a part of the
pays de grandes gabelles, the situation was almost as desperate.
Bloody encounters between smugglers and *gardes* occurred, in
spite of the preventive efforts of the intendant. "Il faut parvenir
à faire de grandes exemples," he wrote to the *contrôleur,* "qui
n'ont pas été faits jusqu'à cette heure parceque le directeur a
poursuivi ces affaires devant le juge des gabelles, jurisdiction
foible, où rien n'avance, sujette à l'appel à la cour des aides.*
He asked an *arrêt d'attribution* giving him power to pass
sentence upon the culprits; and upon receipt of it, he promptly
sentenced one to the gallows and condemned to infamous memory
two others, who had died of wounds received.† Some months
later he sentenced a batch of smugglers, twenty-four in number,
to various punishments: five were sent to the galleys for nine
years, one for life; others were either banished, fined, or sent to
the whipping-post or pillory.‡ Not all the intendants prosecuted
the smugglers so vigorously. De Harouys in Champagne was
particularly lenient toward them, either from kindness of heart
or from indifference, so that he was sharply reprimanded. On
the margin of a letter in which the intendant reported the
sentences passed by him, the *directeur des finances* wrote: "Ecrire
à M. de Harouys que l'indulgence à l'égard de ceux qui commettent le faux-saunage attire de plus grands maux que la sévérité
des jugements. Les édits et déclarations établissent de plus
grandes peines dont on ne doit point se départir."§

The reverse side of this gloomy picture of crime and ruthless
punishment appears from letters of the intendants revealing the
abuses perpetrated by the farmers of the *gabelle* and their
employés. At Moulins, the intendant found the clerks of salt

---

* Boislisle, II. No. 714.
† Boislisle, II. No. 714, note.
‡ Boislisle, II. No. 921, note. Turgot had to contend with similar lawlessness in the
generality of Tours. Boislisle, II. No. 845.
§ Boislisle, II. No. 1308, note. The penalties had been defined by successive edicts.
Smugglers who were convicted of having prosecuted their trade in armed bands of ten
or more were to be condemned to the galleys for nine years; and for life if the offence
was repeated. Cavaliers, dragoons, and soldiers convicted of *faux-saunage* were to be
sent to the galleys. Isambert, XIX. Nos. 956 and 1041.

magazines, in return for an interest in the company, persuading
the measurers to give short weight to the people. Then, too, the
salt sold to the people was often inferior in quality, so that it was
unfit for use. In sheer self-defence the people were forced to
resort to smugglers who could supply them with a better quality.*
Such frauds and abuses, it hardly need be added, were extremely
difficult to detect. Only through sub-delegates and detectives
could the intendant cope with the maladministration that was
only too common.

To the special vigilance of the intendants were recommended
"vagabonds et gens sans aveu." An *arrêt du conseil* of 1673 had
ordered all vagrants to quit the realm within a month, on pain of
condemnation to the galleys.† The intendants were enjoined
"de tenir la main à son entière exécution, n'y ayant rien de plus
important que de purger toutes les provinces de ces sortes de
gens." In this class were included those nondescripts who
went under the name of *Bohêmes*, and who, so far as their
predatory habits are concerned, strongly resemble our gypsies.
The intendants were to treat these *Bohêmes* with the greatest
severity that the law allowed, "Sa Majesté voulant purger son
royaume de toute cette canaille, qui ne sert qu'à tourmenter et
piller les peuples."‡ To this task the intendants addressed themselves with all the greater zeal, since they were well aware that
His Majesty had other reasons than concern for the peace of the
provinces, in desiring these poor beggars to be sent to the galleys.

The Mediterranean flotilla had long been the pet care of
Colbert. To make it more than a match for all opponents was
his constant endeavor, and he had for this purpose sought to
increase the number and size of the galleys, in the fighting
ability of which he had great confidence. The difficulty came in
manning these vessels. No man would voluntarily enter upon
the frightful life of a galley oarsman; slaves could scarcely be
forced into galley service; and when the supply of slaves ran
short, the convicts who filled the loathsome prisons of the land
were pressed into service.§ Even this resource was soon

---

* Boislisle, I. Nos. 408 and 610.
† Colbert, IV. p. 93, No. 83.
‡ Colbert, IV. p. 141, No. 135.
§ One has only to read the accounts of the prisons given by the intendants to
understand why a criminal should prefer the galleys. See Boislisle, II. No. 1001.

exhausted. Few convicts serving their terms in the prisons were fitted for the laborious life of the galleys; the noisome dungeons and scanty, unwholesome fare of the jails wrecked the strongest constitutions. In these straits Colbert sought recruits from among the condemned criminals whom the courts sent daily to prison. Pressure was brought to bear upon the judges to multiply the number of condemnations to the galleys, even if the law had to be strained to make the penalty fit the crime *

The intendants were keenly alive to the needs of the government, and left no stone unturned to curry favor with the king and Colbert. They visited the courts of law to stir up indolent judges; they went through the prisons in search of able-bodied convicts; they scoured the country around for smugglers and vagrants whom they might send summarily to Toulon; they listened for any rumors of sedition that they might pounce upon the offenders. Their letters are full of accounts of how they have made up *"une belle chaisne"* to send to the galleys; they discourse with evident relish upon convicts whom they have discovered to be *"bons hommes et vigoreux et fort propres pour servir,"* etc.†

The intendants were often put to it, to provide for the miserable wretches condemned to the galleys, until the chain gang, on its way to Toulon, should claim them. If economy cautioned against too great expense in feeding them, it also warned against starving them, for many, weakened by hunger, succumbed to the hardship of the fearful march to the coast. If his contingent was sufficiently large, the intendant made up his own gang and committed it to paid conductors, who demanded so high as 80 or 100 livres for every man delivered at Toulon. The losses on the route were frightful.‡ Of 96 men in one chain gang from the generalities of Touraine, Anjou and Orléans, 33 died on the way to Lyons.§ For the horrors of this iniquitous traffic the intendants were only indirectly responsible; they were but the agents of the crown. The spirit animating

---

* Depping. II. p. 910, No. 37.
† Depping. II. p. 874, No. 2; also II. p. 911, No. 37.
‡ Depping, II. p. 875, No. 2. As this was simply a business contract, the conduct of these *conducteurs des chaines* was dictated only by heartless self-interest. The treatment of the unhappy victims was such as to shock the better classes of people even in that age, so accustomed to demoralizing spectacles. See Depping, II. p. 934, No. 30; also II. p. 848, et seq.; also II. p. 881, No. 5.
§ Depping, II. p. 893.

the government appears in a note from the hand of Colbert: "Dans la nécessité présente où le roy est de fortifier les chiourmes des ses galères, c'est une bonne nouvelle pour Sa Majesté qu'il y eust trente bons forçats dans la conciergerie de Rennes......."*

It frequently fell to the lot of the intendant, as the most facile agent of the crown, to aid in the censorship of the press. Louis XIV., who was particularly anxious lest the doctrine of Jansenism should be disseminated through books and tracts, had the intendants institute a general inquiry into the number and resources of publishers and booksellers in their generalities.† One intendant was commissioned to visit the printing offices in Rouen and to arrest any printers in whose possession certain books condemned by the censors were found.‡ Equally unpleasant missions were given to other intendants, as when Bâville was enjoined to keep a sharp lookout for "un libelle manuscrit, très-seditieux," in Languedoc,§ and De Courson was made to search the printing offices of Rouen to find the publisher of Vauban's *Projet de dixme royale.*‖ To such lengths will absolutism go, to stamp out the semblance of resistance!

That system of tutelage over agriculture, manufacturing, and commerce, which the French monarchy had established by the middle of the eighteenth century, and which proved so disastrous to the political and economic independence of the people, was foreshadowed in the reign of Louis XIV. It would have been strange if a government so intrusive in its anxiety for its fiscal affairs had not shown a strong tendency to control and develop those natural resources from which its wealth ultimately was derived; it would have been still more remarkable if that government had not confided many of these new cares to those officers most intimately acquainted with the resources of the provinces.

The extreme solicitude for the state of agriculture that finds expression in repeated letters from the *contrôleurs* to the intend-

* Depping, II. p. 900, No. 25.
† Depping, II. p. 598.
‡ Depping, II. p. 707.
§ Depping, II. p. 846, No. 169. The title was *Avis à tous les alliez protestans et catholiques romains, princes et peuples souverains et sujets, sur le secours qu'on doit donner aux soulevez des Cévennes.* It bore the date 1705.
‖ Depping, II. p. 861, No. 190.

ants can be easily appreciated when one reflects how great the dependence of the people was upon the produce of the soil. To a great degree the amount that the government was to realize from the *taille* depended upon the condition of agriculture. Hence, those innumerable letters, already noted, calling upon the intendants for detailed statements regarding the prosperity or the misfortunes of their generalities. "Do not trust others, see for yourselves," is the often recurring warning of the *contrô-leur*,—and the intendants did see for themselves with astonishing fidelity. Almost insensibly they assumed a tacit guardianship over their generalities, suggesting remedies for the misfortunes of this or that parish, and making themselves petitioners in behalf of the unhappy peasants. One intendant reported a large extent of uncultivated land in his generality, which had been abandoned by the discouraged peasants, and ventured to ask the king to be allowed to distribute seed among them in the hope of persuading them to resume cultivation.* To such requests the king lent a ready ear. Some 60,000 livres were appropriated to purchase grain for seed, but on condition that the recipients should repay the government from the next year's harvest.† "Le Roi," said the prudent Colbert, "répète toujours qu'il n'y a rien de plus dangereux que de laisser croire aux paysans que les plus paresseux seront les plus heureux ou en ne payant pas ou en s'attirant des charités."

A disposition on the part of the government to displace individual initiative by direct control manifested itself increasingly, as the stress of outward circumstance was felt. During the wars of Louis XIV. certain elections on the frontier were forbidden to sow wheat, lest it should furnish sustenance to the enemy in case of invasion; but the inhabitants might sow other cereals ["d'autres petits grains"] for their own support.‡ When the peasants on one occasion refused to sow their fields, for fear of a general famine, the *conseil* issued a general decree, ordering the lands to be sowed as usual; i. e., with the same grains and at the same time as in previous years. The intendants were given authority to carry out the spirit of this decree by special ordi-

* Boislisle, I. No. 585.
† Boislisle, I. Nos. 628, 664.
‡ Boislisle, I. No. 746.

nances of their own.[*] Far more pernicious was the practice of regulating by ordinances the circulation, exportation, and importation of cereals in the provinces. These ordinances always had reference to special localities and to special provinces. They were not dictated by mere caprice, as might appear at first sight, but were based on statistical information, more or less exact, furnished by the intendants. In general, prohibition of the free circulation of grains was the rule; exportation or importation from one province to another was only temporarily and locally permitted.[†] More than one intendant protested against a policy of restriction and interference which he saw meant disaster for his province; but when want came, as it often did come, through the mistaken intermeddling of the government, he could only relieve the people by palliatives. Inasmuch as the ministry assumed the direction of the commerce in grain, the intendant's duties in such matters were largely informatory. He visited the parishes of his generality at least once a year to observe the condition of the crops;[‡] he made careful estimates of the quantity of grain upon reports furnished by his sub-delegates;[§] he watched the market carefully and noted the fluctuations in prices;[||] he kept a sharp lookout for speculators;[¶] and of all these observations he made most minute reports to the *contrôleur général.*

Colbert was particularly desirous of establishing studs for the breeding of cavalry horses, throughout the grazing districts of France. He sent out a commissioner in 1663, to report upon the condition of the studs, and urged the intendants to assist him in every possible way in this matter, which was of such importance to the state.[°] Probably as the result of their efforts, more than 500 stallions were distributed within seven years among the generalities.[f] The care of these *haras* was commended to the intendants in that insistent language so characteristic of the ministers when impressing upon the intendants the importance of new departures.[g]

* Isambert, XX. No. 1521.
+ Monin, *Histoire administrative du Languedoc*, p. 289.
‡ Boislisle, I. No. 1228.
§ Boislisle, I. No. 1230.
  Boislisle, I. No. 1235.
¶ Boislisle, I. No. 1718, note.
° Colbert, IV. p. 206, No. 14.
f Colbert, IV. p. 206, No. 37.
g Colbert, IV. p. 260, No. 104.

The responsibility of the intendants was even greater in connection with the manufacturing interests of France, since the policy of the government was dictated less by precedent and more by the judgment of the intendants. Whenever the government proposed to establish new industries in the country, it almost invariably turned to the intendants to learn what natural advantages for such industries their generalities possessed.* On the other hand, a prospective proprietor of a new industry would very often make the intendant his confidant, hoping through him to reach the ear of the king.† As new industries began to multiply, under the fostering care of Colbert, the duty of encouraging and protecting them devolved more and more upon the intendants; at the same time, as a steadily increasing source of wealth, these industries had to be taken into consideration in estimating the tax-bearing capacity of the people.

Owing to the indifference, or bigotry, of local magistrates, and to natural obstacles, many of these infant industries had a hard struggle for existence. It is interesting to see the personal responsibility that Colbert felt for the success of his policy. "You will do me a special favor," he wrote to the intendants, "if you will be so kind as to take time to make one or two tours of inspection every year."‡ One Van Robais, a Protestant from Holland, who had begun a manufactory of textile fabrics at Abbéville, was the special ward of Colbert, if we may judge from the frequent interchange of letters in regard to him between the *contrôleur* and the intendant of the generality.§ Every two months the intendant, or his delegate, visited the factory to record the number of operatives and to examine the quality and quantity of the goods manufactured. If the need was urgent, the intendant made grants of money to the manufacturer. Such timely aid enabled more than one *entrepreneur* to keep on his feet in hard times. When one mill-owner in Carcassonne fell into straitened circumstances, and was about

---

* Boislisle, I. No. 1057.
  Boislisle, I. No. 1671, note.
  Colbert, II. p. 725, No. 317.
  Colbert, II. p. 731, No. 322.
† Boislisle, I. Nos. 1085, 1481.
‡ Colbert, II. p. 688, No. 282.
§ Colbert, II. p. 743, No. 357.

to go under, the intendant hastened to his aid by recommending that he be given two years to satisfy the claims of his creditors.[*] From encouragement and protection, it was but a single step to regular inspection of these industries. While they were still few and easily inspected, the intendants quite naturally assumed the duty. From time to time Colbert called upon them to visit fairs to observe whether the cloth offered for sale bore the manufacturer's name and the place of manufacture, as the government's regulations required.[†] It was with the intendant at Tours that the idea originated of publicly exposing all defective goods and of attaching to them the manufacturer's name.[‡] The ordinance of the intendant to this effect was approved by Colbert, and afterward incorporated in a general order to the *maires* and *éschevins* of the towns.[§] As the industries developed, the instructions of the *contrôleur* became often very exacting : "Quant à l'article 39 [du règlement général des manufactures], je dois vous dire que, pour en conserver l'exécution et faciliter le débit et l'apprest desdites frocs à Lisieux, vous pourrez rendre vostre ordonnance pour régler le nombre de fils et de portées, et la largeur qu'ils doivent avoir sortant de la main des tisserands, pour revenir à la sortie du foulon à la largeur de demy-aune ordonnée par ledit article........."[‖] Instructions of such import required no small degree of technical knowledge on the part of intendants, and in the course of time a class of intermediate commissioners[¶] grew up, who acted as inspectors under the eye of the intendant. Although the authority of the intendant was still paramount, the instructions of the ministers were couched in somewhat different language: "Vous concerterez, s'il vous plaist, tout ce qui sera nécessaire pour cela avec le commis, les marchands, les facturiers et les juges de police et des manufactures de Laval;" or, "Je vous prie d'examiner cet expédient avec

---

[*] Boislisle, I. No. 1419. Even when the government did not directly subsidize a manufacturer, it often gave him moral support. At Dijon, the town magistrates were urged in almost dictatorial fashion to give "*gratifications*" to fathers who put their children to work in the factories. Colbert, II. p. 688, No. 282.

[†] Colbert, II. p. 559, No. 119.

[‡] Colbert, II. p. 579, No. 165.

[§] Colbert, II. p. 607, No. 196.

Colbert, II. p. 539, No. 119.

[¶] These *commis pour l'exécution des réglemens généraux des manufactures* were to report to the intendants all cases of negligence or disobedience on the part of the local officers. Such the intendants might punish by fine. The *commis* were to report all differences and disputes that arose and the condition of the manufactures in general so that corrective measures might be taken by the intendants or by the *conseil*. Boislisle, I. pp. 558-559.

le commis et les facturiers et de prendre les mesures que vous jugerez les meilleures là-dessus."*

It was probably no meaningless official verbiage when Colbert wrote to the intendant at Riom apropos of public works: "Ce sera une des principales occupations que vous aurez pendant que vous servirez dans les provinces."† A general letter to the intendants urged them to observe, in the course of their regular tours through the generalities, what rivers could be made navigable, and to give an estimate of the work which they considered necessary for that purpose.‡ A similar letter urged them to make the most advantageous contracts possible for the repair of the highways.§ These, it is true, were only a part of the public works undertaken by the state through the agency of the intendants, but they serve to indicate the relation of the intendants to this department of public service.

In the *pays d'élection*, public works were supervised by the intendant, and often executed under his immediate direction. He usually estimated their probable utility and cost: he made accurate report to the *conseil*; he devised ways and means for meeting the expense; and, finally, upon order from the *conseil*, he made the contracts and often provided the materials used in construction.‖ In the *pays d'États* public works were not usually undertaken by the king, but "Sa Majesté peut seulement exciter les deputés aux Estats d'y donner ordre et mesme de faire visiter tous les chemins et faire les réparations nécessaires pour la commodité publique,"¶—rule elastic enough to permit the royal government to put through nearly every scheme that it chose to adopt. With the intendant on hand to see that the work was done "solidement et diligément,"° as he might of right, the projects were usually carried to a successful issue; but left to themselves, the estates either pushed the work only half-heartedly, or abandoned it altogether.¹

* Boislisle, I. No. 1130.
+ Colbert, IV. p. 437, No. 20. Colbert made it a point to write to the intendants once a month about the public works. He earnestly urged the intendants to adopt the same rule. Colbert, IV. p. 537, No. 125.
‡ Colbert, IV. p. 454, No. 38.
§ Colbert, IV. p. 454, No. 39.
‖ Colbert, IV. p. 454, No. 39.
¶ Colbert, IV. p. 501, No. 150.
° Colbert, IV. p. 438, No. 21.
¹ Thomas, *Une province sous Louis XIV*, pp. 185-190.

Indemnity for private property appropriated for state uses was usually fixed *à dire d'experts*,* who were appointed by the intendants in the *pays d'élection*,† and by the claimants themselves or by the estates in the *pays d'états*.‡ All points of dispute between the contractors and private parties, or between the contractors and the government, were adjudicated by the intendant with appeal only to the *conseil*;§ and ordinance power was given to the intendants to settle damages where private individuals had suffered from the construction of new roads and bridges.‖

The government was sublimely indifferent to any opposition to schemes of public improvement. When the people in the generality of Caen protested againt the drainage of certain marshes, Colbert ordered the intendant to secure their consent, or to force them to yield: "Et même si vous avez besoin de quelque autre arrest pour achever entièrement cette affaire, je ne manqueray pas de vous l'envoyer au premier avis que vous m'en donnerez."¶ The whole spirit and history of the old régime is summed up in that sentence.

---

* Dareste, *L'Administration de justice*, p. 136.
† Such is the natural inference, at least, from the correspondence of Colbert.
‡ Thomas, p. 186, Note 1.
§ Dareste, *L'Admin. de justice*, p. 138.
‖ Isambert, XX. Nos. 1955 and 2005.
¶ Colbert, IV. p. 476, No. 65.

BIBLIOGRAPHY.

I.

BOISLISLE, *Correspondance des Contrôleurs généraux des Finances avec les Intendants des Provinces.* 2 vols. Paris, 1874–1883.

DEPPING, *Correspondance administrative sous le règne de Louis XIV.* 4 vols. Paris, 1850–55.

CLÉMENT, *Lettres, instructions, et mémoires de Colbert.* 7 vols. Paris, 1861-65.

CHÉRUEL, *Journal d'Ollivier Lefèvre D'Ormesson.* 2 vols. Paris, 1860.

BAUDRY, *Mémoires de Nicholas-Joseph Foucault.* Paris, 1862.

ISAMBERT, *Recueil général des anciennes lois françaises.* 29 vols. Paris, 1822–27.

BOULAINVILLIERS, *État de la France.* 6 vols. 1837.

BENOIST, *Histoire de l'édit de Nantes;* containing "*Recueil d'édits, Déclarations, Arrêts, Requêtes, Mémoires et autres pièces authentiques*" in volumes I. II. III. and V. Delft, 1693.

II.

AUCOC, *Le Conseil d'État avant et depuis 1789.* Paris, 1876.

CAILLET, *De l'Administration en France sous le ministère de Richelieu.* 2 vols. Paris, 1860.

CHÉRUEL, *Dictionnaire historique des institutions, mœurs et coutumes de la France.* 2 vols. Paris, 1855.

CHÉRUEL, *Histoire de l'administration monarchique en France.* 2 vols. Paris, 1855.

CLÉMENT, *Histoire de Colbert.* 2 vols. Paris, 1874.

DARESTE DE LA CHAVANNE, *Histoire de l'administration en France.* 2 vols. Paris, 1848.

DARESTE R., *La Justice administrative en France.* Paris, 1862.

CLÉMENT, *Le gouvernement de Louis XIV.* Paris, 1848.

CLÉMENT, *La Police sous Louis XIV.* Paris, 1866.

D'AVENEL, *Richelieu et la monarchie absolue.* 4 vols. Paris, 1884–87.

DE BROC, *La France sous l'ancien régime.*

DE TOCQUEVILLE, *L'Ancien Régime et la Révolution.* Paris, 1857.

RAMBAUD, *Histoire de la civilisation française.* 2 vols. Paris, 1888.

III.

BOYER DE SAINTE-SUZANNE, *Les Intendants de la généralité d'Amiens.*

D'ARBOIS DE JUBAINVILLE, *L'administration des intendants d'après les archives de l'Aube.* Paris, 1880.

DUVAL, *État de la généralité d'Alençon sous Louis XIV.*

HANOTAUX, *Les origines de l'institution des Intendants de province.* Paris, 1884.

MARCHAND, *Un Intendant sous Louis XIV.*

MONIN, *Essai sur l'histoire administrative du Languedoc pendant l'intendance de Basville.* Paris, 1884.

BIOGRAPHICAL NOTE.

The writer of the foregoing pages was born at Lowell, Massachusetts, and was prepared for college at the Lowell High School. Entering Amherst College in the autumn of 1888, he pursued courses leading to the degree of Bachelor of Arts, and was graduated in the class of 1892. For two years he was instructor in English and History at the Lawrenceville School, New Jersey, resigning his position to become Roswell Dwight Hitchcock Fellow in History and Political Science at Amherst College during the college year 1894-95. He received the degree of Master of Arts from Amherst College in 1895, the subject of his thesis being a "History of the Executive Patronage." In the summer of 1895 he went to Germany to pursue studies in Political Science and History and matriculated at the University of Leipzig. After spending three semesters at that institution, he entered the "École des sciences politiques" at Paris. Returning to the United States in 1897, he became Fellow in European History at Columbia University in New York City and a candidate for the degree of Doctor of Philosophy. At the present time he is Associate Professor of History in Iowa College, Grinnell, Iowa.

www.ingramcontent.com/pod-product-compliance
Lightning Source LLC
Chambersburg PA
CBHW021642270326
41931CB00008B/1135